AVE MARIA

And Other Great Sacred Solos

41 Songs for Voice and Keyboard

Edited by

Rollin Smith

DOVER PUBLICATIONS, INC.
Mineola, New York

Bibliographical Note

This Dover edition, first published in 2004, is a new compilation of works originally published separately, some of which have been newly engraved. The introduction and notes have been specially prepared by Rollin Smith for this edition.

International Standard Book Number

ISBN-13: 978-0-486-43131-4
ISBN-10: 0-486-43131-2

Manufactured in the United States by Courier Corporation
43131203
www.doverpublications.com

Contents By Composer

Contents By Title

Introduction

The library of sacred vocal solos is vast but, in the words of the American music critic J.W. Henderson, "probably no other field in the broad domain of musical art shows such a heavy growth of weeds." For this collection, therefore, we have sought long and hard for songs of real worth and musical value that are appropriate for places of worship, as well as the home, voice studio, and concert hall.

Those who love sacred music will find a widely varied selection in this volume: from art song settings of sacred texts to excerpts from oratorios, cantatas, and even opera. All have stood the test of time and many remain perennial favorites with congregations across America. We have tried to provide an interesting mixture of music from different countries as well as historical periods and in most instances, the songs are in keys suited to the range of the average voice.

We hope the diversity and quality will make this not only a volume for music lovers but a ready reference for the professional church musician.

Notes on the Music

Although Adolphe Adam (1803–1856) composed some fifty-three comic operas, he is now known almost entirely for his 1841 ballet *Giselle* and the Christmas song *Cantique de Noël,* composed in 1847 and first published with English words in the United States in 1858.

Stephen Adams (1844–1913) was the pseudonym of Michael Maybrick, an English baritone and organist who composed a number of well-known songs, "The Holy City" being his best known.

The two arias by Johann Sebastian Bach (1685–1750) are excerpts from his cantatas. "Jesu, Joy of Man's Desiring" (Wohl mir, daß ich Jesum habe) is from his Cantata No. 147, *Herz und Mund und Tat und Leben,* composed in 1723 for the Feast of the Visitation of the Blessed Virgin Mary. "My Heart Ever Faithful" (Mein Glaubiges Herze) is from the 1724 Cantata No. 68, *Also hat Gott die Welt geliebt* (God So Loved the World).

Two songs by Ludwig van Beethoven (1770–1827) exemplify his religious faith: "The Heavens Declare" and "To Thee, My God," both composed in 1803 and set to religious poems by Gellert. In these settings Beethoven first gave play to his dramatic and emotional impulse and in them the art of the *Lied* was born.

Ernest Guirard set the Intermezzo from Georges Bizet's (1838–1875) *l'Arlésienne* Suite No. 2 to the ordinary of the Latin Mass, "Lamb of God, you take away the sin of the world."

Henri Büsser (1872–1973) was a student in César Franck's organ class at the Paris Conservatoire. He was later choirmaster at the Opéra-Comique (1902–39) and taught composition at the Paris Conservatoire (1930–48). He died on New Years' Eve, just sixteen days short of his 102nd birthday. *The Sleep of the Infant Jesus* was originally composed for organ, harp, and cello. At the composer's request, Charles Raffalli composed a poem to accompany the music.

Since the sixteenth century it was traditional in France to sing a motet in honor of the Blessed Sacrament after the consecration of the host during the Elevation of the Mass. This "Panis Angelicus" is a solo motet composed by Marc-Antoine Charpentier (c.1636–1704), at one time maître de chapelle of Sainte-Chapelle in Paris.

Ernest Chausson (1855–1899) is best known for his *Poème* for violin and orchestra, but he also composed a small amount of religious music, best represented by this exquisite "Ave verum corpus," composed in 1883 while Chausson was still a private composition pupil of César Franck.

The "Cantique de Jean Racine" was probably the piece with which the nineteen-year-old Gabriel Fauré (1845–1924) won first prize in composition at the École Niedermeyer. *En Prière* was written in 1890 as a canticle for voice and organ. The "Pie Jesu" is the solo motet following the Sanctus of Fauré's *Requiem* and was first performed at La Madeleine on January 16, 1888, for the funeral of a noted architect.

Jean-Baptiste Faure (1830–1914) was a famous French opera baritone whose reputation rests today on his two sacred songs, *Le Crucifix* and *Les Rameaux* (The Palms), without a rendition of which many people's Palm Sunday would not be complete.

César Franck (1822–1890) composed a considerable quantity of sacred music but none to equal his "Panis angelicus" composed during the sermon at Sainte-Clotilde on Christmas Day, 1861. The manuscript is in the Library of Congress in Washington, D.C. One of three motets for Benediction, the "Tantum ergo" was written in 1865 for baritone with optional choir; the "Ave Maria," composed around 1880, was first published in February 1889. "La Procession" is one of Franck's finest art songs, composed in 1889 and dedicated to a student, Charlotte Danner, whose father had been Prefect of Strasbourg during the Second Empire.

Charles Gounod (1818–1893) is thought of today as an opera composer, but his reputation during his life rested chiefly upon his religious music. Torn between the pleasures of the flesh and spiritual exaltation, Gounod seemed to find in sacred music an outlet for his mystical aspirations. What has come to be known as the "Bach-Gounod Ave Maria" originated in 1853 as a *Méditation sur le 1er prélude de piano de S. Bach* for a chamber ensemble of violin or cello, piano and organ. *Jésus de Nazareth,* a "chant évangelique" set to words by A. Porte, followed in 1856 and soon appeared in English as "Nazareth." Several pious songs written in English increased Gounod's fame in Britain, among which were "There Is a Green Hill Far Away" (1871) and "Ring Out, Wild Bells" (1880), a setting of verses from Tennyson's *In Memoriam.* "O Divine Redeemer" was Gounod's last sacred song, composed in April 1893, six months before his death. As "Repentir—Scène sous forme de prière" it was originally for mezzo-soprano and orchestra but the accompaniment was arranged for piano by Émile Paladilhe and first published on December 15, 1894 in the literary magazine, *La Revue de Paris.*

Jules Granier's "Hosanna" remains the consummate solo for Easter Sunday and has been recorded by great artists since the earliest days of acoustic cylinders.

Born in France of Irish/Scottish parents, AUGUSTA HOLMÈS (1847–1903) was a pupil of César Franck and the most accomplished female composer to come out of nineteenth-century France. Her famous *Noël* was composed shortly after her conversion to Catholicism in 1900 and sold to the publisher for 250 francs.

LIZA LEHMANN (1862–1918) was a soprano with a three-octave range. After her farewell concert in 1894 she devoted herself to composition, her 1896 song cycle "In a Persian Garden" being a conspicuous success. Among her many songs is the Christmas favorite, "No Candle Was There And No Fire."

FELIX MENDELSSOHN (1809–1847) completed the hymn "Hear My Prayer" on January 25, 1833. A setting of the opening of Psalm 55, it contains the remarkable solo, "O For the Wings of a Dove." The 1926 recording by the choir of London's Temple Church was, by the 1960s, the only church choir record to have sold a million copies.

WOLFGANG AMADEUS MOZART's (1756–1791) song "Contentment" was completed on May 7, 1785; the motet, "Ave verum corpus," presented here in a version for solo voice with accompaniment, was composed at Baden, near Vienna, on June 17, 1791, six months before his death. Although its course is brief and its scale small, its power guarantees it a place in the first rank of the composer's music.

C. HUBERT H. PARRY (1848–1918) was a major figure in British music at the turn of the twentieth century, being the second director of the Royal College of Music and a professor of music at Oxford. His unison song, set to words from William Blake's "Milton," achieved national success in England during and after the First World War. There is a legend in Cornwall and Somerset that as a youth Christ came to England with his uncle, Joseph of Arimathea, who was engaged in the tin trade which then existed between Phoenicia and Cornwall. It is possible that Blake had this legend in mind when he wrote these verses.

MAX REGER (1873–1916) was one of the most prolific latter-day German composers. Among the sixty songs in the six books of the Simple Songs, Op. 76 is this lovely Christmas lullaby set to words by Martin Boelitz.

The "Prayer" from GIOACCHINO ROSSINI's (1792–1868) 1818 opera, *Mosè in Egitto* (significantly revised as *Moïse* for its 1827 Paris Opéra production) is the most famous number from the score. It is sung at the beginning of Act 3 when the Israelites, pursued by the Egyptians, find themselves at the shore of the Red Sea with no way to cross. Moses leads them in a solemn prayer for help.

FRANZ SCHUBERT (1797–1828) wrote more than a thousand works (including 600 songs) in less than eighteen years. Attracted to P. Adam Storck's German translation of Sir Walter Scott's *The Lady of the Lake,* Schubert composed five songs to the verses in 1825, including three of Ellen Douglas's songs, of which this "Hymn to the Virgin" appears in the Third Canto. Each verse begins with the words "Ave Maria" and it was but a short time until someone fitted the Latin text of the prayer, "Hail, Mary, full of grace," to Schubert's immortal melody. The "Litany for All Souls' Day" *(Litanei auf das Fest aller Seelen),* set to words by J.G. Jacobi, was written in August 1818. All Souls' Day follows the Feast of All Saints, celebrated on November 1.

The air misattributed to ALESSANDRO STRADELLA (1642–1682), *Pietà Signore,* having been set to the words "Pie Jesu," was so famous that, in his will, Camille Saint-Saëns expressly forbad its being sung at his funeral. (Some claim it was written in jest by Rossini while others attribute it to Louis Niedermeyer.)

"God Shall Wipe Away All Tears" is from ARTHUR SULLIVAN's (1842–1900) oratorio, *The Light of the World,* which was first performed as the leading feature at the Birmingham Festival on August 27, 1873. The words were selected from the Bible by the composer. In January 1877 Sullivan's elder brother Frederick died and the loss inspired the composition of his most popular song, "The Lost Chord." At the time, Sullivan's songs were as well known as his operettas and his success as a songwriter was never as great as in that year.

The "KOL NIDRÈ," with its marvelously plaintive and touching melody, gradually increasing in volume from pianissimo to fortissimo, is a traditional Hebrew melody sung in the synagogue at the evening service on Yom Kippur, the Day of Atonement.

LOUIS VIERNE (1870–1937) composed the Benediction motet "Tantum ergo" around 1894 while he was assistant to his organ teacher, Charles-Marie Widor, at the Parisian Church of Saint-Sulpice. It is dedicated to the choirmaster of the church.

"Sleeping Christ Child" *(Schlafendes Jesuskind)* was one of two songs written by HUGO WOLF (1860–1903) on October 6, 1888. In all, he set some fifty-three songs to poems by Eduard Mörike within a few months and all were published the following year.

Rollin Smith

Topical Index

AVE MARIA

And Other Great Sacred Solos

O Holy Night

Cantique de Noël

English words by John S. Dwight

ADOLPHE ADAM

new and glor-ious morn!
lui donne un sau-veur,
Fall on your knees!
Peu - ple à ge - noux!
O hear the an-gel
At - tends ta dé-li-
voi - ces! O night di-vine! O night when Christ was
vran - ce! No-ël! No-ël! voi-ci le Ré-demp-
cresc.
born! O night di-vine! O night, O night di-
teur! No-ël! No-ël! Voi - ci le Ré-demp-
rall.
vine!
teur!
a tempo
ff marcato
rall.

mp
2. Led by the light of Faith se-rene-ly beam - ing, With glow-ing
2. De no-tre foi que la lu-miè-re ar-den - te Nous gui-de
mp
hearts by His cra-dle we stand. So, led by light of a star sweet-ly
tous au ber-ceau de l'En-fant. Comme au-tre-fois une é-toi-le bril-
gleam - ing, Here came the wise men from the O-rient land. The King of Kings lay
lan - te Y con-dui-sit les chefs de l'O-ri-ent. Le Roi des Rois naît
pp
pp
thus in low-ly man-ger, In all our tri-als born to be our friend;
dans une hum-ble crè-che, Puis-sants du jour, fiers de vo-tre gran-deur,
cresc.
cresc.

f
He knows our need, to our weak - - ness no stran - ger; Be-
À votre or - gueil c'est de là qu'un Dieu prê - che, Cour-
f
hold your King! Be - fore the Low - ly bend! B-
bez vos fronts de - vant le Ré - demp - teur! Cour-
cresc.
cresc.
hold your King! your King! be - fore Him bend!
bez vos fronts de - vant le Ré - demp - teur!
rall.
rall.
a tempo
ff marcato

mf
3. Tru - ly He taught us to love one an-oth - er; His law is
3. Le Ré - demp - teur a bri - sé toute en - tra - ve; La terre est
mf
love and His gos - pel is peace; Chains shall He break, for the slave is our
li - bre et le ciel est ou-vert. Il voit un frè - re où n'é-tait qu'un es-
pp
broth - er, And in His name all op-pres - sion shall cease. Sweet hymns of joy in
cla - ve, L'a-mour u - nit ceux qu'en-chai-naît le fer. Que lui di - ra no -
pp
grate - ful cho - rus raise we. Let all with - in us praise His ho - ly name!
tre re-con - nais-san - ce; C'est pour nous tous qu'il naît, qu'il souffre et meurt.

f
Christ is the Lord! Then ev-er, ev-er praise we. His
Peu-ple de-bout! chan-te ta dé-li-vran-ce! No-
pow'r and glo-ry ev-er-more pro-claim! His
ël! No-ël! chan-tons le Ré-demp-teur! No-
cresc.
ff
pow'r and glo-ry ev-er-more pro-claim!
ël! No-ël! chan-tons le Ré-demp-teur!
rall.
a tempo
ff marcato

The Holy City

F.E. Weatherly

STEPHEN ADAMS

Andante moderato

Voice

Piano

p

Last

night I lay a - sleep - ing, There came a dream so fair, I
then me-thought my dream was changed, The streets no long - er rang,

stood in old Je - ru - sa - lem, Be - side the tem - ple there; I
Hushed were the glad Ho - san - nas The lit - tle chil - dren sang; The

heard the chil - dren sing - ing, And ev - er as they sang, Me -
sun grew dark with mys - ter - y, The morn was cold and chill, As the
mf cresc.
thought the voice of an - gels, From heav'n in an - swer rang, Me -
shad - ow of a cross a - rose Up - on a lone - ly hill, As the
f
cantabile
thought the voice of an - gels From heav'n in an - swer
shad - ow of a cross a - rose Up - on a lone - ly
dim.
rang. Je - ru - sa - lem, Je - ru - sa - lem,
hill. Je - ru - sa - lem, Je - ru - sa - lem,
p

mf
Lift up your gates and sing,
Hark how the an - gels sing,
Ho - san - na in the
mf
high - est, Ho - san - na to your King!
f
colla voce
ff a tempo
dim.
1
p
And
2
affret. poco a poco
And once a-gain the scene was changed, New earth there seemed to be, I
pp

saw the Ho - ly Ci - ty Be - side the tide - less sea; The
light of God was on its streets, The gates were o - pen wide, And
cresc.
f
cantabile
all who would might en - ter, And no one was de -
dim.
nied. No need of moon or stars by night, Or
p

affret.
sun to shine by day, It was the new Je -
cresc.
allargando
ru - sa-lem That would not pass a - way, It
f
allargando
grandioso
rall.
was the new Je - ru - sa - lem That would not pass a -
f
rall.
p
a tempo
way. Je - ru - sa - lem, Je -
3
p a tempo

cresc.
ru - sa-lem! Sing for the night is o'er! Ho -
cresc.
mf
san - na in the high - est, Ho - san - na for ev - er -
mf
f
ad lib.
more! Ho - san - na in the high - est, Ho -
f
colla voce
san - na for ev - er - more!
ff

Jesu, Joy of Man's Desiring

Wohl mir, daß ich Jesum habe

Martin Jahn
Translated by Robert Bridges

JOHANN SEBASTIAN BACH

wis - dom, Love most bright,
Drawn by
Thee, our souls as - pir - ing
Soar to
un - cre - a ted light.

Word of God, our flesh that
fash - ion'd With the fire of
life im - pas - sion'd.
2
2

Striv - ing still to Truth un - known,
Soar - ing, dy - ing round Thy throne.
3

My Heart Ever Faithful

Mein gläubiges Herze

JOHANN SEBASTIAN BACH

Je - sus ist nah!
Je - sus is near!
mf
dim.
Weg Jam - mer, weg Kla - gen, weg Jam - mer, weg Kla - gen, ich
A - way — with com-plain - ing, a - way — with com-plain - ing, Faith
will — euch nur sa - gen, mein Je - sus ist da; weg Jam-mer, weg Kla-gen, ich
ev - er main-tain - ing, My Je - sus is here; A - way with com-plain-ing, Faith
poco cresc.
dim.
p
will — euch nur sa - gen, mein Je - sus ist da, mein — Je - sus ist da;
ev - er main-tain - ing, My Je - sus is here, my — Je - sus is here;
mf
weg
A-
cresc.

Jam - mer,weg Kla - gen,weg Jam - mer,weg Kla - gen,ich will_ euch nur sa - gen,mein
way_with com-plain - ing, a - way_with com-plain - ing,Faith ev - er main-tain - ing, My
p
Je - sus ist da! Mein gläu - bi-ges Her - ze, froh - lo - cke,sing', scher-ze,
Je - sus is here! My heart_ev-er faith - ful, Sing prais - es, be joy - ful,
mf
mein gläu - bi-ges Her - ze, froh -
My heart_ev-er faith-ful, Sing
p
dim.
lo - cke,sing', scher - ze,froh - lo - cke,sing', scher - ze, dein Je - sus ist da, froh -
prais - es, be joy - ful,sing prais - es, be joy - ful, Thy Je - sus is here, Sing

lo-cke, sing', scherze, froh - lo - - - cke, sing', scher - -
praises, be joy-ful, sing prais - - - es, be joy - -
dim.
- - ze, mein gläu - bi-ges Her - ze, froh - lo - cke, sing', scher - ze, froh -
- - ful, My heart_ev-er faith-ful, Sing prais - es, be joy - ful, sing
p
lo - cke, sing', scher - ze, dein Je - sus ist da!
prais - es, be joy - ful, Thy Je - sus is here!
mf
cresc.
f

The Heavens Declare His Glory Eternal

Die Ehre Gottes aus der Natur: *"Die Himmel rühmen des Ewigen Ehre,"* Op. 48, No. 4

Gellert

LUDWIG VAN BEETHOVEN

cresc.
placed in Heaven the bright shin-ing star? A-long the
cresc.
sky, who guides the sun? Who bids him dart forth his
pp
cresc.
f
beams from a-far, And glo-rious-ly his cour-ses run, and
fz
p
f
fz fz
glo-rious-ly his cour-ses run?
ff
fz
fz fz
ff

To Thee, My God

Gott, deine Güte reicht so weit, Op. 48, No. 1

Gellert

LUDWIG VAN BEETHOVEN

Though oft Thy ways are wrapt in
Herr! mei - ne - Burg, mein Fels, mein
clouds, in clouds mys - te - rious and un - known,
Hort, ver - nimm mein Fleh'n, merk' aus mein Wort;
Truth,
Den
Righ - teous - ness, and Mer - cy shall stand The pil - lars
ich will vor dir be - ten, den ich will vor dir
of Thy throne.
be - - ten.
p
cresc.
f
decresc.
pp

Agnus Dei

Intermezzo from *l'Arlésienne Suite* No. 2

Arranged by Ernest Guirard

GEORGES BIZET

mi - se - re - re, mi - se - re - re no - bis.
O, have com - pas - sion, have com-pas - sion up-on us.
sf
dim.
A - gnus De - i! qui tol - lis pec - ca - ta mun - di,
Lamb of God, thou that tak - est a - way the world's guilt,
sf
dim.
3
p
cre - scen - do
mi - se - re - re, mi - se - re - re, mi - se - re - re
Have com-pas - sion, have compas - sion, have com-pas - sion up -
p
cre - scen - do
f
f
p
no - bis. A - gnus, A - gnus De - i! qui tol - lis pecca - ta
on us. Lamb of God, Lamb of God, thou that tak - est away the
p

cresc. molto.
mun - di, A - gnus, A - gnus De - i! qui tol - lis pecca - ta
world's guilt, Lamb of God, Lamb of God, thou that tak - est a-way the
cresc. molto.
dim.
cresc. molto.
mun - di, do - na no - bis pa - cem. A - gnus De - i! do - na
world's guilt, may thy peace be with us. Lamb of God, may thy
dim.
cre - scen - do molto.
allargando.
pa - cem. A - gnus De - i! do - na no - bis pa - cem.
peace, thy peace be with us, may thy peace be with us,
allarg.
ritenuto molto.
Do - na no - bis, Do - na pa - cem.
Thy peace, thy peace, may thy peace be with us.
ritenuto molto.

à Monsieur Hébert, de l'Institut

Le Sommeil de l'Enfant Jésus

The Sleep of the Infant Jesus

Berceuse pour la nuit de Noël

1896

Charles Raffalli

HENRI BÜSSER

a Tempo 1º
dolce.
fraì - - - che. Dor - - mez, Pe_tit Jé_
a Tempo 1º
p
bien soutenu.
pp
Ped.
✳ Ped.
_sus! Dor - - mez, doux ché_ru - bin!
✳ Ped.
✳
Vo_tre mè_re vous gar - - - de Et veille au_près_de
Ped.
✳ Ped.
✳ Ped.
✳
pp
dolce.
vous. Dor - mez! Nos
cresc.
dim.
p
Ped.
✳ Ped.
✳ Ped.
✳ Ped.
✳ Ped.
✳

cœurs pleins d'espé _ ran _ _ _ ce Ont foi dans votre a _
_ mour! Re _ po _ sez douce _ ment, Jé _ _
_ sus, bien cher en _ fant! Dor _ mez!
A Dieu di _ sons no _ tre joie! No _
pp
p
mf
cresc.
dim.
f
Ped.

p
mf
f
ad lib.
-ël! chantons No-ël! No-ël! chantons toujours No-ël! No-ël! No-ël!
pp subito.
cresc. molto.
f
Ped.
dolce. a Tempo 1º
No-ël! Fê-te bé-nie! Ô jour de déli-
riten.
a Tempo 1º
dim.
pp
-vran-ce! Un Sauveur vient de naî-tre, Nous voi-ci tous à ses ge-
-noux. No-ël! Mi-
misterioso
pp
cresc.
dim.
pp sost.

Un poco più lento.
_nuit... tout est mys _ tè _ _ re! Tout dort autour de
Un poco più lento.
Ped.
nous!
Re_ _po_sez douce_ment, Ô Jé _ _
pp rit. poco.
ad lib.
pp
suivez bien.
_sus! Bien cher en _ fant! Dor _ mez! Dor _
a Tempo.
p
dolcissimo.
pp
cresc.
dim.
rit.
a Tempo.
_mez, doux ché _ ru _ bin, Que de leurs blan _ ches
pp misterioso.
pp
Ped.

ai - les Les an-ges, croi-sant leurs mains frè - les, A -
(FA ♭)
pp
Ped.
cédez un peu.
mf
p
-bri-tent vo-tre front di - vin! Dor - mez! Dor -
suivez.
p e dim. sempre.
Lent.
a Tempo.
ad lib.
pp
-mez, doux ché-ru - bin! No - ël! No -
pp suivez.
mf vibrato.
dim.
ppp
-ël! No - ël!
ppp

Panis Angelicus

Élévation à voix seule

MARC-ANTOINE CHARPENTIER

ser-vus, et hu - mi-lis. O, O O res mi-ra - bi
lis! O, O, O res mi - ra - bi-lis! man-du-cat
Do - mi-num Pau - per, ser-vus, et hu - mi-lis. O res mi-
ra - bi-lis! O, O, O res mi - ra - bi - lis!

Ave Verum Corpus

Op. 6, No. 2

ERNEST CHAUSSON

pp a Tempo.
A - ve ve - rum cor - pus Na_tum de Ma - ri - a
a Tempo.
Un peu plus vite.
Vir - gi - ne
Un peu plus vite.
p
Cu - jus la -
- tus per_fo - ra - - tum, Un -
cresc.
m.d.
m.g.
cresc.
- da flu - xit cum san - gui - ne Es -
cresc.
- to no - bis prœ - gus - ta - tum mor - tis in e -
cresc.

-xa - - mi - ne:
p
rit.
Tempo 1º
cresc.
f
O Je-su dul - cis, O Je - su pi - e, O Je-su,
Je - su, fi - li Ma - ri - - æ,
pp
3
Tu no - bis mi-se-
-re - re, Tu no - bis mi-se - re - re, Tu no-bis mi-se-
-re - - re
en retardant.
A - - - men:

à Monsieur Cesar Franck

Cantique de Jean Racine

Op. 11

Jean Racine

GABRIEL FAURÉ

p
Verbe é - gal au Très-Haut notre
pp
sempre legato
u - nique es - pé - ran - - ce, Jour é - - ter - - -
- nel de la terre et des cieux, De
pp
p

la pai - si - ble nuit nous rom - pons le si -
cresc.
- len - - ce, Di - vin Sau - - - veur, jet -
cresc.
f
- te sur nous les yeux, Di - vin Sau -
f
dim.
p
- veur, jet - te sur nous les yeux!
dim.
p

dolce.
Ré - pands sur
pp
p
nous le feu de ta grâ - - ce puis - san - - te, Que

cresc.
f
tout l'en - - - fer, que tout l'en - fer fuie au son
cresc.
f
p subito.
de ta voix, Dis - si - - pe le som - meil d'une
p subito.
mf
â - me lan - guis - san - - te Qui la con -
mf
- duit à l'ou - bli, à l'ou-bli de tes lois,

f
Qui la con - duit à l'ou - bli, à l'ou-bli de tes
f
lois! O Christ, sois fa - vo - rable à ce
p
p
sempre legato.
peu - ple fi - dè - le, Pour te bé -
- nir, main - te - nant ras - sem - blé, Re -
cresc.

cresc.
_çois les voeux qu'il offre à ta gloire___ im _ mor _
cresc.
cresc.
f
_tel _ _ le, Et de___ tes___ dons___ qu'il re _
f
pp subito.
_tour _ _ ne com _ blé! Et de___ tes___
pp subito.
p
dons___ qu'il re _ tour _ _ ne com _ blé!
p

dolce.
Et de tes
dons qu'il re - tour - ne com - blé qu'il re -
pp
poco rall.
- tour - - - - ne com - blé!
pp

à Mme Leroux-Ribeyre

En Prière

Stéphan Bordèse

GABRIEL FAURÉ

cresc.
lois Sur la ter - - re, Je sau - rai Vous ser -
cresc.
- vir au - gus - te Roi des rois. Ô lu - miè - - re!
f
f
p
Sur mes lè - vres, Sei - gneur met - tez la vé - ri - té Sa - lu -
p
- tai - - re Pour que ce - lui qui doute, a - vec hu - mi - li -
mf

_té Vous ré _ vè _ _ re! Ne m'a_ban_don_nez
pas, don_nez-moi la dou _ ceur Né_ces _ sai _ _ re,
Pour a _ pai _ ser les maux, sou_la_ger la dou _ leur, La mi_
_sè _ _ _ _ re! Ré _ vé _ lez - Vous à
Sempre dolce

moi, Sei - gneur en qui je crois Et j'es -
- pè - - - re Pour Vous je veux souf -
- frir et mou - rir sur la Croix au cal - vai -
- re!
Poco rit.
Poco rit.
a Tempo

Pie Jesu

from

Requiem, Op. 48

GABRIEL FAURÉ

un poco più
mf
Pi - e Je - su Do - mi - ne do - na — e - is
meno p
mf
dim.
p
re - qui-em do - na e - is re - qui - em
dim.
pp et très
dolce
Do - na — do - na
lié
sempre pp

Do - - mi-ne do-na e - is re - - qui-em
poco cresc.
sem - pi - ter - nam re - - qui - em
p
sem - - pi-ter - nam
re - - qui-em
pp
sem - pi-ter - nam re - - qui-em
pp

mf
Pi - e Pi - e Je - - su Pi - e Je - su do - mi-ne
mf
do - na e - is do - na e - is sem - - pi - ter - - nam
très lié
pp
re - - qui-em sem - pi - ter - nam re - qui - em.
poco ritenuto
poco ritenuto

Crucifix

Translated by Theodore T. Barker

JEAN-BAPTISTE FAURE

All ye that suf - fer, come to Him, And taste his grace!
Vous qui souf - frez, ve - nez à lui: car il guè - rit.
Your trembling hearts be - fore Him place,
Vous qui tremblez, ve - nez à lui,
Come, where He waits with smil - - - ing face!
ve - - nez à lui: car il sou - rit.
mf
cres.
col canto
rall.
cres.
dim.
Come, when the hour of death draws nigh: He ev - er liv - - eth! He ev - er
Vouz qui pas - sez, ve - nez à lui: car il de - meu - - re, car il de -
marcato
rall.

liv - - - - - - - eth! In life's last hour on Him re - ly Who lives for -
meu - - - - - - - re. Vous qui pas - sez ve - nez à lui: car il de -
mf
cres - - - cen - - - - do
ev - - - er! Come, when the hour of death is nigh! He ev - er
meu - - - re, Vous qui pas - sez ve - nez à lui: car il de -
f
liv - - - - eth! He lives for - ev - - - - er!
meu - - - - re, car il de - meu - - - - re,
ff
dim.
rall. pp
He lives for - ev - - - - er!
car il de - meu - - - - re.
p
rall.
dim.
pp

The Palms

Les Rameaux

JEAN-BAPTISTE FAURE

Where Je - sus comes to wipe our tears a - way,
Hu - man - i - ty to each doth give his right,
Through bound - less love the Christ of Beth - le - hem,
E'en now the throng to wel - come him pre - pare;
While those in dark - ness find re - stored the light;
Brings faith and hope to thee for - ev - - er more;
cresc.
ff allargando
a tempo
Join all and sing, His name de-clare,
mf
Let ev - 'ry voice re - sound with ac - - cla-ma - tion, Ho -
p
cresc.

san - - - na! praise ye the Lord!
ff
Bless him who com-eth to bring us sal - va - - - -
3
3
allargando
f
tion!
f
1.2.
3. last time
r.h.

Ave Maria

CÉSAR FRANCK

p
A - ve Ma - ri - a, gra - ti - a ple - - na;
a tempo
p
Do - mi - nus te - cum: be - ne - - dic - ta tu
poco cresc.
in mu - li - e - ri - bus, et be - ne - dic - tus
poco cresc.
cresc.
et be - ne - dic - tus fruc - tus ven - tris tu - i
cresc.

poco rit.
dim.
a tempo
dolce
Je - - sus
Sanc - ta Ma - ri - a,
f dim.
pp
dolce
cresc.
Ma - ter De - i,
O - ra pro no - bis
cresc.
dim.
pec - ca-to - ri-bus,
nunc et in ho - ra
f
dim.
dolce
p
mor - tis nos - træ.
Sanc - ta Ma -
dolce
p

cresc.
ri - a, Ma - ter Dei - i, o - ra pro -
cresc.
f
dim.
no - bis pec - ca - to - ri - bus, nunc et in ho - ra
f
dim.
rit.
p a tempo
pp
mor - tis nos - træ A - - men
rit.
a tempo
p
pp
A - - men.
rit.

Panis Angelicus

CÉSAR FRANCK

O loving Father, Thee would we be praising
Dat panis coelicus figuris termi-
sempre legato
alway. Help us to know Thee, know Thee and
num. O res mirabilis manducat
sempre legato
love Thee; Father, Father, grant us Thy truth and
Dominum, Pauper, pauper, servus et humi-
p
cresc.
f

p
cresc.
grace; Fa - ther, Fa - ther, guide and de - fend
lis, Pau - per, pau - per, (f) ser - vus et hu - mi -
p
us.
lis.
mf
mf
un poco cresc.
Rule Thou our wil - ful hearts, Keep Thee our
Pa - nis an - ge - li - cus fit pa - nis
dim.
cantabile con molto espr.

, più cresc.
(,)
dim.
wan-d'ring thoughts; In all our sor - rows let us find our rest in
ho - mi - num (f) Dat pa - nis coe - li - cus fi - gu - ris ter - mi -
poco cresc.
cresc.
dim.
Thee; And in temp - ta - tion's hour, Save through Thy
num, O res mi - ra - bi - lis man - du - cat
cresc.
, f cresc.
might - y pow'r, Thine aid O send us; Hear
Do - mi - num, Pau - per, pau - per, ser -
f

dim.
(9) f
us in mer - cy.
Show us Thy
- vus et hu - mi - lis,
Pau - - per,
dim.
molto cresc.
f
un poco dim.
rall.
fa - vor, So shall we live, and sing praise to
pau - per, ser - vus, (9) ser - vus et hu - mi -
un poco dim.
rall.
Thee.
lis.
a tempo
rall.

à Madame Charlotte Danner

La Procession

Charles Brizeux

English version by Nathan Haskell Dole

CÉSAR FRANCK

fields a-long! O'er the meadows, and the moors, green beech-en wood-lands
vers les champs! Par les lan-des, les — prés, les verts tail-lis de
poco cresc.
rift - ed. He comes by hosts at-tend-ed
hê - tres. Il vient, sui-vi du peu-ple
largamente
mf
dim.
pp
meno dolce
by the priests high up-lift - ed; Oh ye birds, add your car - ols To
et por-té par les prê - tres: Aux can-ti-ques de l'hom - me, oi -
meno p
cresc.
man's — a-dor-ing song! — It is end-ed.
seaux, — mê-lez vos chants! — On s'ar-rê-te.
cresc.
pp

The throng a - bout an oak as - sem - bling
La foule au - tour d'un chêne an - ti - - que
In sol - - emn awe in - cline Be - fore the mys - tery
S'in - cline, - - en a - do - rant, sous l'os - ten - soir mys-
poco più f
dim.
trem-bling. Oh Sun! pour down thy rays Up - on this hal-lowed
ti - que: So - leil! dar - de sur lui tes longs ray - ons cou -
poco rit.
cresc.
a tempo
shrine!
chants!
dim.

molto dolce
Oh, ye birds, add your car - - - ols, To
Aux can - ti - - ques de l'hom - - - - me, oi
pp
man's a - dor - - ing song!
-seaux, mê - lez vos chants!
cresc.
Fair flowers, your breath com - -
Vous, fleurs, a - vec l'en - -
cresc.
-bine With the in - cense up - well - ing! Oh
cens ex - ha - lez votre a - rô - me! O
con forza

splen - dor! all is light, And prayer and praise-high-
fê - te! tout re - luit, tout prie et tout — em -
f
poco rall.
swell - - - - ing!
bau - - - - me!
ff
poco rall.
molto dim.
a tempo
molto dolce
God is mov-ing the fields a - long.
Dieu s'a-vance à tra - vers les champs.
a tempo
pp
poco rall.
God is mov-ing the fields a - long.
Dieu s'a-vance à tra - vers les - champs.
poco rall.

à Sophie Kapeler

Tantum Ergo

CÉSAR FRANCK

cresc.
f
dim.
p
ti - quum do - cu - men - tum No - vo ce - dat ri - - tu - i;
cresc.
f
dim.
p
più f
dim.
dolce
Prae - stet fi - des sup - ple - men - tum Sen - su - um de - fe - ctu -
più f
dim.
dolce
i.
dolce
Ge - ni - to - ri, Ge - ni - to - que Laus — et
dolce

pp
ju - - bi - la - - - ti - - o, Sa - - - lus, — ho - nor,
pp
poco rit. dim.
vir - - tus — quo-que Sit — et be - ne - di - - - cti - o;
poco rit. dim.
più f
Pro - - - ce - - den - - ti ab u - - tro-que Com - par sit lau -
più f
p
p
dim.
da - ti - o. A - men, A - men.
dim. rall.

Ave Maria

Meditation on Bach's First Prelude

CHARLES GOUNOD

Thou happy mother,
gra - ti - a ple - na,
Ped. cresc.
Ped. pp
God is with thee,
Do - mi - nus te - cum,
Ped. cresc.
Ped. pp
Bless - ed, bless - ed art
be - ne dic - ta
Ped. cresc.
Ped.
thou A - bove all
tu in mu - li
Ped.
Ped. cresc.

moth - ers, Since in Beth - le-hem,
e - ri-bus et be - ne-dic - tus
p
cresc.
p
came to thee the an - gel of the
fruc - tus ven - tris tu - i Je -
cresc.
dim.
Lord Hon - or'd and bless - ed,
sus Sanc - ta Ma-ri - a,
p
cresc. molto
f
hon - or'd and bless - ed Ma-ri - a
sanc - ta Ma - ri - a Ma-ri - a
cresc. molto

Moth - er of Je - sus In - fant Re -
O - ra pro no - bis, no - bis pec-ca -
Ped. pp
Ped.
Ped. molto cresc.
deem - er, Born to save us from our
to - ri-bus, nunc et in ho - ra in
Ped.
Ped.
Ped. ff
sins and all our heav-y woes
ho - ra mor-tis nos-trae A -
Ped.
Ped.
Ped. dim.
A - men.
ve! A - ve!
Ped. p
Ped. pp
Ped.

Nazareth

Jésus de Nazareth

CHARLES GOUNOD

Life for ev - er - more
dim.
p
cresc.
dim.
mf
Shep - herds who fold - ed your flocks be - side you,
Tell what was told by an - gel voi - ces near: "To
f
you this night is born He who will guide you Thro'

paths of peace to liv-ing wa-ters clear."
pp
colla voce
p
Tho' poor be the cham-ber, Come here, come and a-dore,
p
Lo! the Lord of Hea-ven Hath to mor-tals giv-en
cresc.
dim.
cresc.
dim.
Life for ev-er-more.
p
p
p
p
cresc. dim.
p

Kings from a far land, draw near, and be-
hold Him, Led by the beam whose
warn - ing bade ye come, Your crowns cast
tr
p cresc.
down, with robe roy - al en-

pp
fold Him Your King de - scends to
dim.
pp
pp
earth from bright - er home
colla voce
rit.
pp
Tho' poor be the
pp a tempo
cham - ber Come here, come and a - dore;
Lo! the Lord of Hea ven Hath to mor - tals
cresc.
dim.
cresc.

giv - en Life for ev - er - more.
dim.
p
p
p
cresc.
dim.
p
Wind to the ce - dars pro-claim the joy - ful
p
sto - ry, Wave of the sea, the

ti - dings bear a - far The night is
p
gone! Be - hold in all its glo - ry All
broad and bright ri - ses th'E - ter - nal Morn - ing
rit.
f
rit.
Star Tho' poor be the cham - ber, Come
ff

here, come and a - dore, ___ Lo! the Lord of
Hea - ven Hath to mor - tals giv - en
dim.
Life for ev - er - more, Life for ev - er -
p
more, ___ Life for ev - er - more! ___
cresc. rit.
cresc. rit. dim.
p

O Divine Redeemer

Repentir

CHARLES GOUNOD

p
tir! — À mon ai - de, Sei - gneur, — hâ - te - toi d'ac - cou -
ne! — Do - mi - ne De - us me - us, De - us for - tis et
tress! — Answer me from thy throne, — haste Thee, Lord, to mine
p
p cresc. cresc. dim.
rir — et prends pi - tié — de ma dé - tres - se! et prends pi - tié — de ma dé -
potens! qui - a pec - ca - vi, in te spe - ra - vi, par - ce pec - ca - tis, De - us
aid, — Thy pit - y show — in my deep anguish! Thy pit - y show — in my deep
p cresc. dim.
p cresc.
tres - se! De la jus - ti - ce ven - ge - res - se Dé - tour - ne les coups, mon Sau -
me - us! Ad te cla - ma - vi, ad te con - fu - gi, in mi - se - ri - cor - di - â
anguish! Let not the sword of vengeance smite me, tho' righteous thine an - ger, O
cresc. cresc.
cresc. f
veur! De la jus - ti - ce ven - ge - res - se Dé - tour - ne les coups, mon Sau - veur! —
tu - â! Do - mi - ne De - us, Deus me - us! in mi - se - ri - cor - di - â tu - â!
Lord! Shield me in dan - ger, O re - gard me! On Thee, Lord, a - lone will I call. —
p cresc. f

p
O di - vin Rédemp - teur!
A - ni - ma me - a,
O, di - vine Re - deem - er!
O di - vin Ré-demp -
A - ni - ma me -
O, di - vine Re -
p
teur! par - donne à ma fai - bles - se, par -
a spe - ra - vit in Do - mi - no, spe - ra -
deem - er! I pray Thee, grant me par - don, and re -
cresc.
cresc.
dim.
don - ne, pardonne à ma fai - bles - se!
vit a - ni - ma, a - ni - ma me - a!
mem-ber not, re-mem-ber not my sins!
p
par -
Spe -
For -
dim.
p
p
don - ne! O di - vin Ré-demp - teur! par -
ra - vit a - ni - ma me - a, spe -
give me, O, di - vine Re - deem - er! I

cresc.
donne à ma fai - bles - se, par - don - ne, pardonne à ma fai -
ra - vit in Do-mi - no, spe - ra - vit a - ni - ma, a - ni - ma
pray Thee, grant me par - don, and re - member not, re - member not, O
cresc.
ad lib.
dim.
bles - se!
me - a!
Lord, my sins!
Dans le se-cret des nuits
Am - pli-us la - va me
Night gathers round my soul;
colla voce
dim.
a tempo
je ré-pandrai mes pleurs,
et a pec-ca - to me - o,
fear - ful, I cry to Thee;
je meur-tri-rai ma chair
et a pec-ca - to me - o
Come to mine aid, O Lord!
sous le poids du ci - li - ce;
mun-da me, Do - mi - ne,
Haste Thee, Lord, haste to help me!
cresc.
et mon cœur,
Do - mi - ne
Hear my cry,
cresc.

dim.
p
al - té - ré du sanglant sa - cri - fi - ce,
De - us me - us, De - us for - tis et po - tens,
hear my cry! Save me, Lord, in Thy mer - cy;
dim.
p
bé - ni - ra de ta main les clé - men - tes ri -
munda me, Do - mi - ne, a pec - ca - to me -
hear my cry, hear my cry! Come and save me, O
poco rit.
p a tempo
gueurs! O di - vin Ré - demp - teur!
o! A - ni - ma me - a,
Lord! O, di - vine Re - deem - er
poco rit.
p a tempo
O di - vin Rédemp - teur! par - donne à ma fai -
a - ni - ma me - a spe - ra - vit in Do - mi -
O, di - vine Re - deem - er! I pray Thee, grant me
cresc.
cresc.

dim.
bles - se, par - don - ne, pardonne à ma fai - bles -
no, spe - ra - vit a - ni - ma, a - ni - ma me -
par - don, and re - member not, re-member not, O Lord, my
dim.
p
De la jus - ti - ce ven - ge - res - se Dé -
se!
In tu - â jus - ti - ti - â, in
a!
Save, in the day of ret - ri - bu - tion, from
sins!
p
p
cresc.
tour - ne les coups, mon Sau - veur! O di - vin Rédemp - teur! par -
mi - se - ri - cor - di - â tu - â, de pre - ca - ti - o - nem ex -
Death shield Thou me, O my God! O, di - vine Re - deem - er, have
p
cresc.
f
poco rit.
ad lib.
dim.
pp
don - ne à ma fai - bles - se!
au - di! in te spe - ra - vi!
mer - cy! Help me, my Sav - ior!
l. h.
dim.
f
poco rit.
colla voce
pp
pp

Ring Out, Wild Bells

Alfred Lord Tennyson

CHARLES GOUNOD

Ring out, wild bells, and let him die.
Ring out the old, ring in the new,
Ring, hap - py bells, a - cross the snow.
The year is go - ing, let him go;
Ring out the false, ring in the true.
cresc.
dim.
p
mf
cresc.
f

Ring out the grief that saps the mind, For those that
p
here we see no more; Ring out the feud of rich and poor,
cresc. molto
Ring in re - dress to all man - kind. Ring out the
f
dim.
mf
want, the care, the sin, The faith-less cold-ness of the times.

cresc.
Ring out, ring out my mournful rhymes,
But ring the full - er minstrel
cresc.
in:
Ring out old shapes of foul dis - ease;
Ring out the
nar-row-ing lust of gold;
Ring out the thou-sand wars of old,
con 8va
allargando poco
a tempo
gloriously
Ring in the thou-sand years of peace.
Ring in the val-iant man and
colla voce

free,
The larg-er heart, the kind-lier hand,
Ring out the darkness of the land,
Ring in the Christ,
ring in the Christ,
ring in the Christ that is to be,
ring in the Christ that is to be.
ff
poco rit.
a tempo
rit.
a tempo

There Is a Green Hill Far Away

Le Calvaire

Mrs. C.F. Alexander

CHARLES GOUNOD

Where the dear Lord was cru - ci - fied, Who died to save us
Où le Sei-gneur, bon - té di - vi - ne, Mou - rut pour l'hu - ma - ni -
cresc.
dim.
all.
té.
We may not know, we can - not tell, What
Et sans sa - voir, sans pouvoir dire Tout
p
cresc.
pains He had to bear,
ce qu'il a souf - fert,
But we be - lieve it
Nous croy - ons que par
dim.
p
cresc.
was for us He hung and suf - fer'd there.
son mar - tyre Le ciel nous fût ou - vert!
He
Il
dim.
p

died that we might be for - giv'n, He died to make us good,
meurt pour que Dieu nous par - donne, Oui, c'est pour nous qu'il meurt,
cresc.
dim.
p
That we might go at last to Heav'n, Sav'd by His precious blood.
Et notre cé - les - te couron - ne Est le prix de ses dou-leurs.
cresc.
dim.
p
There was no oth - er good e - nough — To pay the price of
Par quelle of - fran - de as-sez for - te De nos fau - tes nous la-
p
sin, He only could un - lock the gate Of
ver? Lui seul du ciel pou - vait ou - vrir la
p
cresc.

molto espress.
Heav'n and let us in. O dear - ly, dear - - - ly has He lov'd, And we must love Him, too, And
por - te Et nous sau - ver. Il nous ai-ma, Il nous ai - ma, nous de - vons donc l'ai - mer Et
f
dim.
p
trust in His re - deeming blood, And trust in His re - deeming blood, And try His works to do, and
croire à la ver - tu fé - conde Du Christ; il a sau - vé le monde Et nous de - vons l'i - mi - ter, oui,
p
cresc. molto
dim.
p

try His works to do!
nous de - vons l'imi - ter!
p
We must love Him, too!
nous de - vons l'ai - mer!
p
We must love Him, too, And try His works to
nous de - vons l'ai - mer, oui, nous de - vons l'ai -
dim. p
do!
mer!
pp

Hosanna

Julien Didiée
English version by Isabella G. Parker

JULES GRANIER

cresc.
ing, Mourn ye no more, Joy - ful be -
tre, Ne pleu - res plus, Lè - ves les
cresc.
p
hold Bright ser - a - phim In their glo - ry un - told
yeux Les sé - ra - phins il - lu - minent les cieux.
rit.
marcato il canto
rit.
p
a tempo
p
Un poco animato
p
In the hea - ven - ly re - gions Hear me - lo - di - ous le - gions.
Dans la sphère a - zu - ré - e C'est leur voix in - spi - ré - e
marcato la melodia
cresc.
f
Him for ev - er they bless, Je - sus Christ they con - fess.
Qui bé - nit le Sei - gneur Jé - sus Christ ré - demp - teur.
f
cresc.
L.H.
rit.

Maestoso
Christ, my heart thou en - fold - est
O Jé - sus, tu m'em - bra - ses
Thou my soul ev - er hold - est.
de cé - les - tes ex - ta - ses,
By Thy grace I see Thy face!
Je te vois O di - vin roi!
Ho - san - na! Ho - san - na! Ho - san - na! All shall raise,
Ho - san - na, Ho - san - na, Ho - san - na, gloire à toi,
Ho - san - na, glo - ry, praise!
Ho - san - na, gloire à toi!
cresc.
allarg.
molto rit.
rall.

Un poco più lento
p
Night dark - ly veiled all the day's glo - ry When on - the
La som - bre nuit voi - lait en - co - re Du fils de
trem.
pp
earth closed the sad sto - ry, Now doth the sun beam bright once
Dieu la sainte au - ro - re, Mais le so - leil a res - plen -
cresc.
f
more While all the world doth in wonder a - dore.
di et l'u - ni - vers se prosterne é - blou - i
marcato il canto
dim.
rit.
a tempo
ff

Un poco animato
In the midst of the angels, the angels and archangels,
Au milieu des phalanges Des anges, des archanges
la melodia ben marcato
L.H.
cresc.
See the Victor on high Resplendent in the sky!
Voyez-le s'avançant Sublime et triomphant
rit.
Maestoso
Christ, my heart Thou enfoldest,
O Jésus, tu m'embrases,
Thou my soul ever holdest.
de célestes extases,

cresc.
By Thy grace I see Thy face, Ho-
Je te vois, ô di-vin roi Ho-
f
cresc.
san-na! Ho-san-na! Ho-san-na! All shall
san-na, Ho-san-na, Ho-san-na, gloire à
allarg.
raise, Ho-san-na, glo-ry, praise!
toi, Ho-san-na, gloire à toi.
ff molto rit.
ff
f rall.
ff a tempo

Noël

Trois anges sont venus ce soir

Moderato.

VOICE. *p*

PIANO. *p*

Three Angels came to me this night Bearing incense, treasures and posies! One held a gold-en cen-ser bright, And an - other a crown of ros-es; The third one held out a broider'd gown Which seem'd too sacred to carry; With pearls and buds it was flower'd down Like the robes of our La-dy Ma-ry! "No - ël! No-ël! We do love thee well And for

Trois anges sont ve - nus ce soir M'appor - ter de bien bel - les choses; L'un deux a - vait un en - censior, L'autre a - vait un chapeau de ro - ses, Et le troisième a - vait en main U - ne ro - be tou-te fleu-ri-e De per - les, d'or et — de jasmin, Comme en a Ma-da-me Ma - ri - e! _No - ël! No-ël! Nous ve - nons du ciel T'appor-

più f

più f

più f

p
thee these gifts did bor-row, For God on high, In the bright blue sky! Is quite
ter ce que tu dé - si - res, Car le bon Dieu Au ford du ciel bleu Est cha-
p
sad, when He sees thee sor - row!"
grin lors - que tu sou - pi - res!
p
p
"Wilt thou the gold - en censer swing And wear the rose - crown
Veux - tu le bel en - cen-soir d'or, Ou la rose é - close en cou-
p
fragrant? Or take the snow-white robe we bring With a cir-clet of sil-ver brilliant? Or
ron - ne? Veux - tu la robe, ou bien en - cor Un col - lier où l'argent fleu - ron - ne? Veux-
p

taste the fruit from the Ho-ly store, Or_ corn of ce-lestial_ reaping, Or like the shepherds of
tu des fruits du ___ Pa-ra-dis Ou du blé des cé-les-tes_ granges? Ou comme les ber -
più f
olden lore See the In-fant Je-sus_ sleeping? "No-ël! No-ël! I do thank ye well, But fair
gers, ja-dis, Veux-tu voir Je-sus dans ses lan-ges?_ No-ël! No-ël! Retour-nez au ciel, Mes beaux
p
Angels speed a - bove!_ In His bright blue sky, Beg of God on high Bliss and
an-ges à l'instant mê-me; Dans le ciel bleu De-man - dez à Dieu Le bon-
p
joy for the one I love!_
heur pour ce-lui que j'ai - me!
p
dim.

No Candle Was There And No Fire

Frances M. Gostling

LIZA LEHMANN

born,
In the stall where our Sav - iour was
laid
Till the ro - sy - red break - ing of
morn,
cresc.
For the Christ-child and Sav - iour no
mf
colla voce
light,
dim.
and nev - er a can - dle to

burn.
p dolce.
cresc.
But the
moon gave a ra - diance di - vine,
And the
stars an ef - ful - gence bright;
And the

p
on - ly sound to be heard Was the
cresc.
low - ing of kine through the night, And the
cresc.
f rall.
pp poco rall.
sigh - ing of wind in the trees, and the
L.H.
colla voce.
f
flap - ping of An - gels' wings.
pp poco rall.

O For the Wings of a Dove

from
Hear My Prayer

W. Bartholomew, Esq.

FELIX MENDELSSOHN

ff
sf
f
wil-derness build me a nest, And re-main there for-ev-er at rest, In the
Wü-ste eilt' ich dann fort, fän-de Ru-he am schat-ti-gen Ort, In die
dim.
p
wil-derness build me, build me a nest, And re-main there for-ev-er at rest,
Wü-ste eilt' ich, eilt' ich dann fort, fän-de Ru-he am schat-ti-gen Ort,
f
dim.
p
In the wil-der-ness build me a nest, And re-main there for-ev-er at rest,
In die Wü-ste eilt' ich dann fort, fän-de Ru-he am schat-ti-gen Ort,
And re-main there for-ev-er at rest, And re-main there for-ev-
fän-de Ru-he am schatti-gen Ort, fän-de Ru-he am schat-
-er at rest. O for the wings, for the
-ti-gen Ort. O könnt' ich flie-gen wie
mf cresc.

wings of a dove, the wings of a dove, Far a - way, far a -
Tau - ben da - hin, wie Tau - ben da - hin! Weit hin - weg vor dem
way would I rove, Far a - way would I rove, a -
Fein - de zu fliehn, vor dem Fein - de zu fliehn, dem
way would I rove, far a way, In the wil - der - ness
Fein - de zu fliehn weit hin - weg! In die Wü - ste
build me a nest, And re-main there for - ev - er at rest, And re -
eilt' ich dann fort, fän-de Ru - he am schat-ti-gen Ort; fän - de
f
main there for - ev - er at rest, re - main there for - ev - er at
Ru - he am schat - ti - gen Ort, hin - weg vor dem Fein-de zu

cresc.
rest, re - main there for - ev - er at rest, O for the wings, for the
fliehn, hin - weg vor dem Fein - de zu fliehn, O könnt' ich flie - gen wie
p
wings of a dove, Far a - way, far a - way would I rove, O, for the wings, for the
Tau - ben da - hin! weit hin - weg vor dem Fein - de zu fliehn! O könnt' ich flie - gen wie
cresc.
f
wings of a dove, Far a - way, far a - way, far a - way, far a -
Tau - ben da - hin, weit hin - weg, weit hin - weg, weit hin - weg vor dem
cresc.
way would I rove, In the wil - der - ness build me a nest, And re -
Fein - de zu fliehn! In die Wü - ste eilt' ich dann fort fän - de
cresc.
f
main there for - ev - er at rest, In the wil - der - ness build me
Ru - he am Schat - ti - gen Ort, In die Wü - ste eilt' ich,

dim.
p
f
build me a nest, And re-main there for - ev - er at rest, In the wil-der-ness
eilt' ich dann fort, fän-de Ru - he am schat-ti-gen Ort, In die Wü - ste
build me a nest, And re-main there for - ev - er at rest, for - ev - er at rest,
eilt' ich dann fort, fän-de Ru - he am schat-ti-gen Ort, am schat-ti-gen Ort,
f
for-ev - - - er at rest, And re-main there for - ev - er at rest,
am schat - ti-gen Ort, fän-de Ru - he am schatti-gen Ort,
p
And re-main there for - ev - - er at rest.
fän-de Ru - he am schat - ti-gen Ort.

Contentment

Die Zufriedenheit, K. 473

Christian Felix Weisse

WOLFGANG AMADEUS MOZART

Ave Verum Corpus

K. 618

WOLFGANG AMADEUS MOZART

dim.
per - fo - ra - tum Ve - ro flu - xit - san - gui - ne:
dim.
pp
cresc.
E - sto no - bis - prae - gu - sta - tum In mor - - tis ex -
pp
cresc.
f
a - mi - ne, in mor - - - - - - -
f
dim.
p
pp
- tis ex - a - mi - ne.
tr
dim.
p
pp

Jerusalem

Op. 208

William Blake

C. HUBERT H. PARRY

mf
poco cresc
seen? And did the Coun - ten-ance Di-vine Shine forth up - on our cloud-ed
mf
poco cresc.
f
poco rit.
hills? And was Je - ru sa-lem build - ed here A-mong those dark Sa-tan - ic
f
poco rit.
mf
mills?
Bring me my
f
ff
mf
8
bow of burn-ing gold! Bring me my ar-rows of de sire! Bring me my
8

spear! O clouds un - fold! Bring me my Cha - ri - ot of
Fire! I will not cease from men - tal fight; Nor shall my
sword sleep in my hand Till we have built Je - ru - sa -
- lem In Eng-land's green and plea - sant land.
p
p
Allargando
ff
ff
rit.
rit.
ff
8

The Virgin's Slumber Song

Mariä Wiegenlied
from
Schlichte Weisen, Op. 76, No. 52

Martin Boelitz
English version by Edward Teschemacher

MAX REGER

p
And soft and sweet - ly sings a bird up - on the bough:
Zu ih - ren Fü - ssen singt ein bun - tes Vö - ge - lein:
pp
pp
Ah, ba - by, dear one,
Schlaf,' Kind - lein, sü - - - - sse,
ppp (una corda)
espress.
rit.
dolciss.
slum - - ber now!
schlaf' nun ein!
rit.
a tempo
dolciss.
espress.
p
Hap - py is Thy laugh - ter, ho - ly is Thy
Hold ist dein Lä - cheln, hol - der dei - nes
p
espress.

si - lent rest, Lay Thy head in slum - ber,
Schlum - mers Lust, leg dein mü - des Köpf - chen
pp
fond - ly on Thy Moth - er's breast! Ah,
fest an dei - ner Mut - ter Brust! Schlaf,
pp
espress.
ppp dolciss.
ba - by, dear one,
Kind - lein, sü - sse,
rit.
dolciss.
slum - ber now!
schlaf' nun ein!
rit.
dolciss.
ppp

Preghiera

from

Moses

GIOACCHINO ROSSINI

po - pol tuo pie - tà
- nie - der auf dein Volk!
peu - ple gé - mis - sant.
6
6
Se pron - tialtuo po - te - re son e - - te-meu - tie
Du führst das Heer der Ster - ne durch dei - nes Him - mels
a - près un long o - ra - ge con - duis nous au ri -
sfe - re: tua-mi - co scam - po ad di - ta al dub - bio erran - te
Fer - ne, er - leucht' auch uns - re Pfa - de durch dei - nes Lich - tes
- va - ge et sau - ve du nau-fra - ge tes fi - dè-les hé -
pie Pie - to - so Dio nea i - tà! noi non ri - viam chein -
Schein, er - leucht' auch uns - re Pfa - de durch dei - nes Lich - tes
- breux con - duis nous au ri - va - ge ob - jet de tous nos

_te. Schein. vœux
In Dem ô
ques _ to cor do len _ te deh! scen _ dioh Dio cle _ men _ te! e
hof _ fenden Ge_mü_the ent _ hül _ le dei _ ne Gü _ te, mit
toi que tout ré_vè _ re aux cieux et sur la ter _ re é
far _ ma_co so_a _ ve di pa _ ce ren _ di al sen! Il
dei _ ner Pal _ me We _ hen ver _ scheu _ che un _ sern Schmerz, mit
_cou _ te ma pri_è _ re pro _ té _ ge tes en _ fans ô
no _ stro cor, che pa _ ve deh tu con_for _ ta al men!
dei _ ner Pal _ me We _ hen ver _ scheu _ che un _ sern Schmerz.
toi que tout ré_vè _ re é _ cou _ te nos ac _ cens

Dal tuo stella _ _ to
Der du das All um_
des cieux où tu ré_
sog _ lio, Sig _ nor ti vol _ gia no _ _ i, pie _ tà de fi _ gli
_ fas _ sest mit dei _ nen Va _ ter _ ar _ _ men, o bli _ cke mit Er_
_ si _ des grand Dieu toi qui nous gui _ des de tes en_fans ti_
tuo _ i del po _ pol tuo pie _ tà! po _ pol tu _ o pi _ e_
_ bar _ men her _ nie _ der auf dein Volk, mit Er_bar _ men auf dein
_ mi _ des _ ter _ mi _ ne les re _ vers. Dieu ter_mi _ ne nos re_
_ tà po _ pol, po _ pol tu _ o pi _ e _ tà!
Volk, mit Er_bar_men auf dein fle _ hend Volk.
_ vers Dieu ter_ mi _ ne nos re _ vers.

Ave Maria

Op. 52, No. 6

Sir Walter Scott
English adaptation of Adam Stork's German translation
by Dr. Theodore Baker

FRANZ SCHUBERT

wild, 'Tis Thou, 'tis Thou canst save a - mid de-spair. We
wild soll mein Ge-bet zu dir hin-we - - hen. Wir
na, A - ve, A - ve! Do-mi-nus, Do-mi-nus te-cum. Be-ne-
slum - ber safe-ly till the mor - row, Tho' e'en by men out-cast, re-vil'd: O
schla - fen si-cher bis zum Mor - gen, ob Men - schen noch so grausam sind: O
di - cta tu in mu - li - e - ri-bus, et be - ne-di - - ctus, et
Maid - en, see a maid-en's sor-row, O Moth - er, hear a suppliant child!
Jung - frau, sieh' der Jung-frau Sor-gen, o Mut - ter, hör' ein bit-tend Kind!
be - ne - di - ctus fru - ctus ven-tris, ven-tris tu - i, Je - - sus.
fp
pp
A - - ve Ma - ri - - -
A - - ve Ma - ri - - -
A - - ve Ma - ri - - -

a!
a!
a!
A - ve Ma-ri - - - - a! Un - de -
A - ve Ma-ri - - - - a! Un - be -
A - ve Ma-ri - - - - a! Ma - ter_ De -
fil'd! The flint - y_couch where-on we're sleep - ing Shall seem with down of ei - der
fleckt! Wenn wir auf die - sen Fels hin-sin - ken zum Schlaf, und uns dein Schutz be-
i, O - ra pro no - bis pec-ca - to - ri-bus, O - ra, o-ra pro no -
pil'd, If_ Thou a - bove sweet watch art keep - - ing. The
deckt, wird weich der har - te Fels uns dün - - ken. Du
bis, O - ra, o - ra_ pro no - bis_ pec-ca-to - ri-bus, nunc,

murk - y cav - ern's air so heav - y Shall
lä - chelst, Ro - sen-düf - te we - hen in
et in ho - ra mor - tis, in
breathe of balm, if Thou hast smil'd; O Maid - en, hear a maid-en plead-ing, O
die - ser dumpfen Fel - sen-kluft; o Mut - ter, hör' des Kin-des Fle - hen, o
ho - ra mor-tis no - stræ, in ho - ra mor-tis, mor-tis no-stræ, in
Moth - er, hear a suppliant child! A - ve Ma-ri - - - -
Jung - frau, ei - ne Jung-frau ruft! A - ve Ma-ri - - -
ho - ra mor-tis no - stræ. A - ve Ma-ri - - -
a!
a!
a!

A - ve Ma-ri - - - a! Stain - less
A - ve Ma-ri - - - a! Rei - ne
A - ve Ma-ri - - - a! gra - ti-a ple -
styl'd! All fiends of-air or earth-ly es - sence, From this their wonted haunt ex-
Magd! Der Er - de-und der Luft Dä-mo - nen, von dei - nes Au-ges Huld ver-
na, Ma-ri - a, gra - ti-a ple - na, Ma-ri - a, gra-ti-a ple-
il'd, Shall flee be-fore Thy ho-ly pres - - ence! We
jagt, sie kön - nen hier nicht bei uns woh - - nen! Wir
na, A - ve, A - ve! Do-mi-nus, Do-mi-nus te cum; Be-ne-
bow, be-neath our cares o'er-la - den, To
woll'n uns still dem Schick - sal beu - gen, da
di - cta tu in mu - li - e - ri-bus, et

Thy dear guid - ance rec - on-cil'd; Then
uns dein heil - 'ger Trost an-weht; du
be - ne - di - - - ctus, et
hear, O Maid, a sim - ple maid-en, And for a fa - ther hear a child!
Jung - frau wol - le hold dich nei - gen dem Kind, das für den Va - ter fleht!
be - ne - di - ctus fru - ctus ven - tris, ventris tu - i, Je - sus.
fp
pp
A - ve Ma - ri - - - - a!
A - ve Ma - ri - - - - a!
A - ve Ma - ri - - - - a!
dim.

Litany for All Souls' Day

Johann Georg Jacobi

FRANZ SCHUBERT

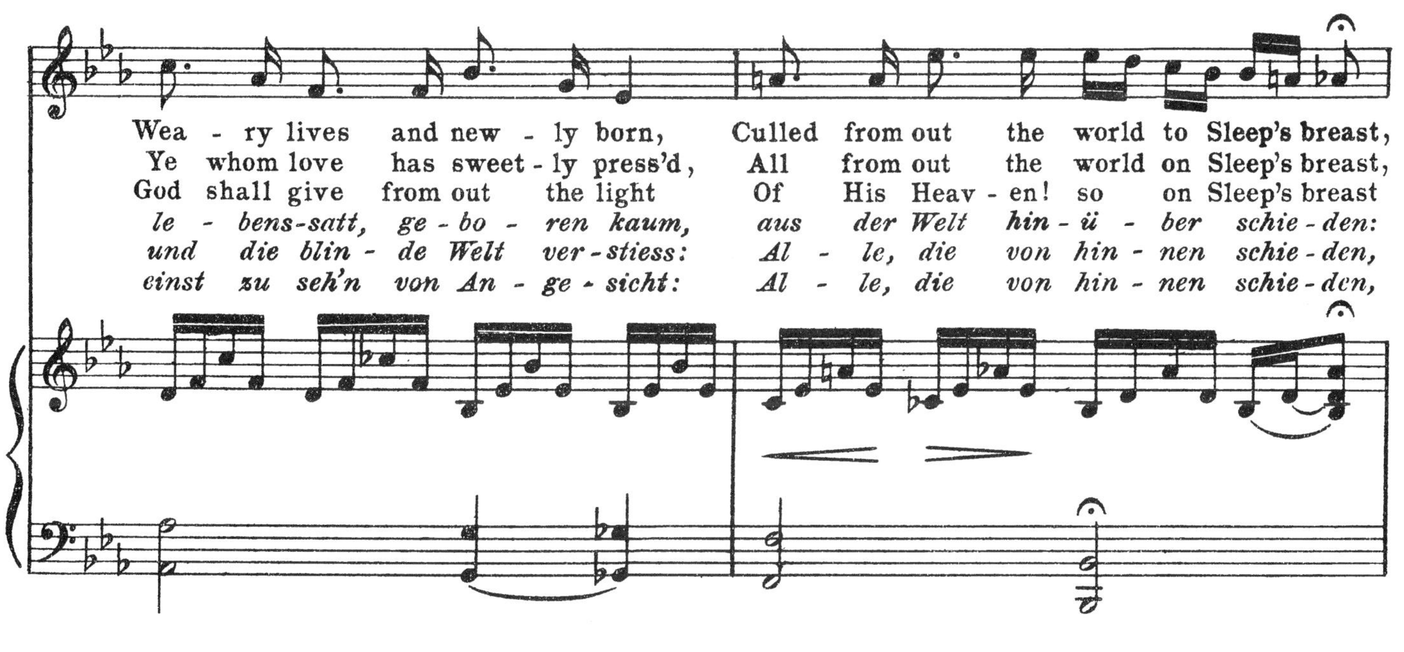
Wea - ry lives and new - ly born, Culled from out the world to Sleep's breast,
Ye whom love has sweet - ly press'd, All from out the world on Sleep's breast,
God shall give from out the light Of His Heav - en! so on Sleep's breast
le - bens-satt, ge - bo - ren kaum, aus der Welt hin - ü - ber schie - den:
und die blin - de Welt ver - stiess: Al - le, die von hin - nen schie - den,
einst zu seh'n von An - ge - sicht: Al - le, die von hin - nen schie - den,

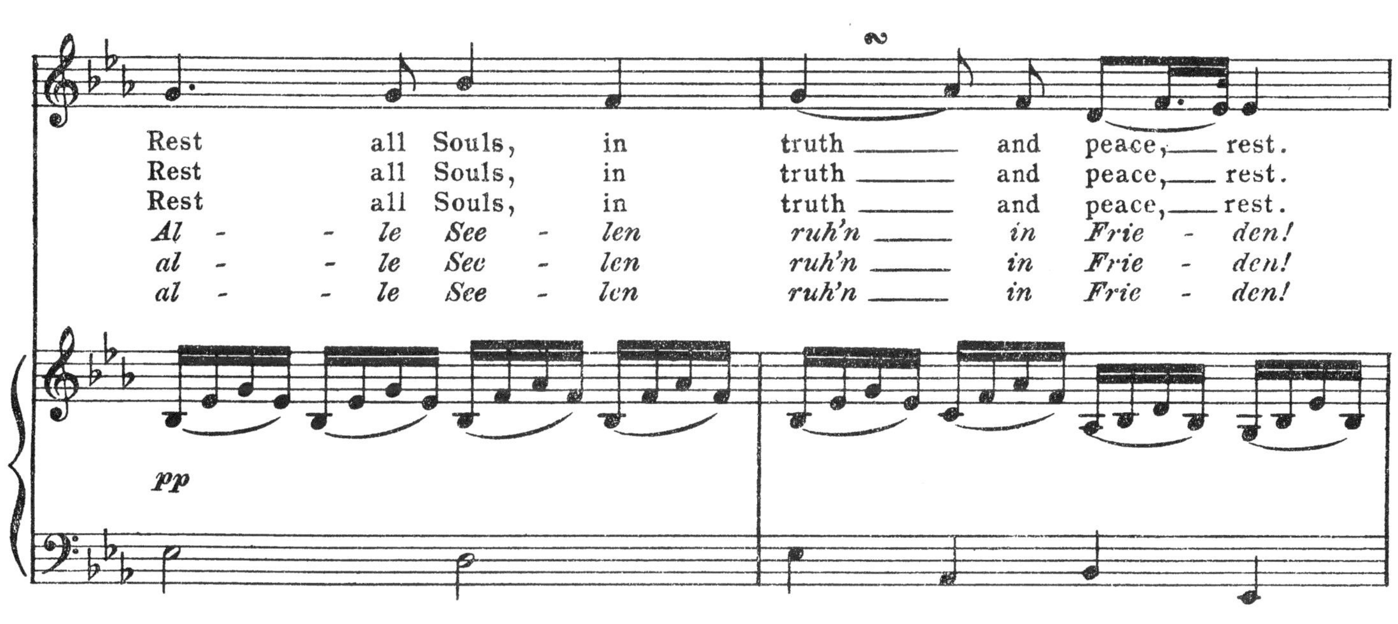
Rest all Souls, in truth and peace, rest.
Rest all Souls, in truth and peace, rest.
Rest all Souls, in truth and peace, rest.
Al - le See - len ruh'n in Frie - den!
al - le See - len ruh'n in Frie - den!
al - le See - len ruh'n in Frie - den!
pp

cresc.

Pietà, Signore

O Lord, Have Mercy

English version by Harrison Millard

Attributed to ALESSANDRO STRADELLA

pp
mf
Non mi pu - ni - sca il tu - o ri - gor, Me - no se - ve - ri,
Let not the hand with rig - or fall, Be wrath-ful nev - er,
cresc.
f
p
cle-men-ti o - gno - ra, Vol-gi i tuo - i sguar-di so - pra di me,
for - giv - ing ev - er, Shed Thy light up - on me, Lord, heed my call,
cresc.
so - pra di me. Non fi - a ma - i che nel - l'in - fer - no
O heed my call! My I ne'er mer - it, That in per - di - tion
dim. rit. a tempo
Si - a dan - na - to nel fuo-co e - ter - no Dal tu - o ri - gor.
My soul may lan - guish, But may con - tri - tion, And Thy grace heal all.

p
cresc. molto
Gran Di - o, giam - ma - i si - a dan -
Je - ho - vah, O nev - er may I be
cresc.
f
dim.
na - to nel fuo - co e - ter - no Dal tu - o ri - gor, dal tuo ri -
tor - tured by fires e - ter - nal, for Ad - am's first fall, for Ad - am's
gor.
fall.
tr
Pie - tà, Si - gno - re,
O Lord, have mer - cy,
Si - gnor, pie - tà di me do - len - te,
Lord, hear my pray'r; I call up - on Thee,

se a te giun - ge il mio pre - ga - re, il mio pre - gar,
Grant me Thy bless - ing, show me Thy fa - vor, hear Thou my pray'r,
p
cresc.
Me - no se - ve - ri, cle - men - ti o - gno - ra, vol - gi i sguar - di
Be wrath - ful nev - er, For - giv - ing ev - er, Shed Thy light on me,
p
deh vol - gi i sguar - di su me, Si - gnor, su me, Si - gnor.
shed Thy light on me, and heed my call, heed Thou my call.
Pie - tà, Si - gno - re,
O Lord, have mer - cy,

cresc.
di me do - len - te!
my soul is heav - y,
Si - gnor, pie - tà, —
Lord, hear my call,
se a te giun - ge il
Grant me Thy bless - ing,
p
cresc.
dim.
pp
mi - o pre - gar,
hear — my pray'r,
Non mi pu - ni - sca il tu - o ri - gor,
Let not Thy hand with rig - or fall,
mf
f
p
Me - no se - ve - ri, cle - men - ti o - gno - ra
Be wrath - ful nev - er, For - giv - ing ev - er,
Vol - gi i tuo - i sguar - di so - pra di
Shed Thy light up - on me, and hear my
cresc.
me, so - pra di me;
call, Lord, heed my call,
Non fi - a ma - i che nel - l'in -
May I ne'er mer - it That in per -

cresc.
dim.
fer - no Si - a dan - na - to nel fuo - co e - ter - no Dal
di - tion My soul may lan - guish, But may con - tri - tion And
tr
p
tu - o ri - gor, Gran Di - o! Giam -
Thy grace heal all. Je - ho - vah, O
cresc.
rall.
ma - i si - a dan - na - to nel fuo - co e - ter - no dal
nev - er may I be tor - tured by fires e - ter - nal, for
tu - o ri - gor, dal tuo ri - gor.
Ad - am's first fall; may grace heal all.
dim.

God Shall Wipe Away All Tears

from *The Light of the World*

Sir Arthur Sullivan

SIR ARTHUR SULLIVAN

ARIA. Andante moderato.
♩ = 88.
The Lord is ri - - - sen, He will dwell with
men, and they shall be his peo - - ple! and God shall
wipe a - way all tears from their eyes, There shall be no more
death, nei - ther sor - row nor cry - ing, nei - ther shall there be

a.‐ny more pain. God shall wipe a‐way all tears from their
p
eyes, There shall be no more death, nei‐ther sor‐row nor cry‐ing,
f
nei‐ther shall there be a‐ny more pain, For the for‐mer things are
f
meno f
pass'd a‐way. Be‐hold I make all things new, saith the
meno f

f
Lord, For the former things are pass'd away. Behold I make
f
meno f
all things new, saith the Lord,
dim.
saith the
dim.
rall.
p a tempo.
Lord. God shall wipe away all tears from their
rall.
pp
eyes, There shall be no more death, neither sorrow nor crying,
cres
cres

cen - - - - do
nei - - ther shall there be a - ny more pain, and God shall
f
cen - - - - do
wipe a - way all tears, all tears from their eyes. There shall be
p
dim.
no more death, nei - ther sor - row nor cry - ing, nei -
p
cres.
rall.
- - ther sor - row nor cry - ing!
rall.
p colla voce
Ped. *

The Lost Chord

Adelaide Procter

SIR ARTHUR SULLIVAN

Andante moderato

p *cresc.* *f* *dim.* *p*

Seat-ed one day at the or-gan, I was wea-ry and ill at ease, And my

p

fin-gers wan-der'd i-dly O-ver the noi-sy keys; I know not what I was

cresc.

play-ing, Or what I was dream-ing then, But I struck one chord of mu-sic, Like the

cresc. *dim.* *p*

cresc.
f
poco rall.
dim.
sound of a great A - men, Like the sound of a great A - men.
cresc.
f
dim.
p cresc.
f
dim.
It flood - ed the crim - son twi - light, Like the close of an An - gel's
p
cresc.
Psalm, And it lay on my fe - ver'd spir - it, With a touch of in - fi - nite
dim.
cresc.
dim.
cresc.
dim.
calm, It qui - et - ed pain and sor - row, Like love o - ver - com - ing strife, It
cresc.
dim.

tranquillo sempre
seem'd the har-mo-nious ech - o From our dis-cord-ant life, It link'd all per-plex-ed
p
p tranquillo
poco a poco più animato
mean-ings In-to one per - fect peace, And trem-bled a-way in-to si-lence, As
cresc. animato
f agitato
if it were loth to cease; I have sought, but I seek it vain-ly, That
f agitato
f
one lost chord di - vine, Which came from the soul of the or - gan, And

grandioso
f
en - ter'd in - to mine. It may be that Death's bright Angel, Will
cresc. molto ritard. f
ff
speak in that chord a - gain; It may be that on - ly in Heav'n I shall hear that grand A -
sempre ff
men, It may be that Death's bright An - gel, will speak in that chord a - gain, It
ff
sf sf
fff
ritard. con gran forza
may be that on - ly in Heav'n I shall hear that grand A - men.
ritard. colla voce. con gran forza
a tempo
rallentando

Kol Nidrè

Traditional

rim - na, v'- di - a - sar - na al al -
f
3
pp
naf - sha - ta - na mi - yom ki - pu - rim ze ad -
f
yom ki - pu - rim ha - bah
dolce
p
a - lè - nu l'- to - vah,

pp e dolce
f
Ko - l' - hon ich - rat - na v' - hon, kol - hon y' - hon sha - ran.
pp
mf
Sh'vi - kin, sh' - vi - tin b' - tè - lin, u-m'- vu - ta - lin, la sh'- ri -
p
pp
rin v'- la kay-ya - min. Nid - ra - na la nid -
f
p
rè ve'e - sa-ra - na la e - sa - rè u - sh'vu-a - ta - na la sh' - vu - ot.

à Philippe Bellenot, maître-de-chapelle de Saint-Sulpice

Tantum Ergo

Op. 2

LOUIS VIERNE

dim.
poco a poco
rall.
a Tempo
Sen - su - um de - fec - tu - i.
Ge - ni - to - ri
a Tempo
poco a poco
rall.
poco cresc.
dim.
cresc. poco a poco
Ge - ni - to - que Laus et ju - bi - la - ti - o
Sa - lus ho - nor vir - tus quo - que
poco cresc.
dim.
cresc.
poco a poco
dim.
cresc.
Sit et be - ne - dic - ti - o
Pro - ce - den - ti ab u - tro - que Com - par sit lau -
dim.
cresc.
dim. poco a poco rall.
dim. e poco rall.
- da - ti - o Com - par sit lau - da - ti - o
A - men A - men.
dim. poco a poco rall.
dim. e poco rall.

Sleeping Christ Child

Schlafendes Jesuskind

Eduard Mörike

HUGO WOLF

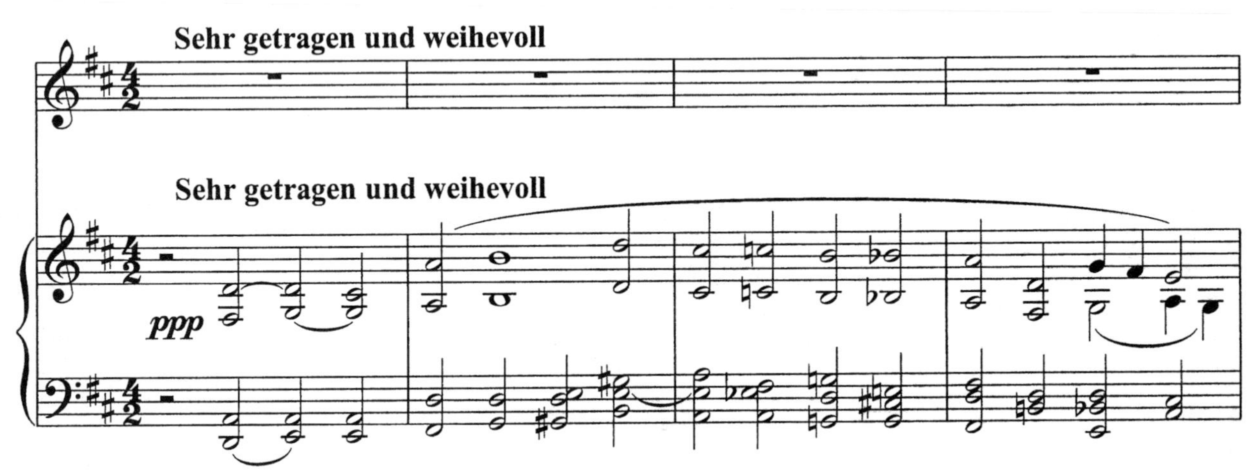

3
mu - sing, gave Thee as a fit - - ting pil - low for Thy
sinn - voll spie - lend dei - nen leich ten Träu - men un - ter -
dream - ings;
leg - te;
sehr ausdrucksvoll
3
flow' - ret Thou, e'en in the
Blu - me du, noch in der
bud en - fold - ed bear - - est Thou the glo - ry of the
Knos - pe däm - mernd ein - - ge - hüllt die Herr - lich - keit des
Fa - ther.
Va - ters!
sehr innig
If one could but pic - ture
O wer se - hen könn - te
p
mf

all the won'-drous vi-sions seen be-hind that brow, those
wel che Bil-der hin-ter die-ser Stir-ne, die-sen
zart
long dark lash-es, chang-ing oft in sweet suc-ces-sion.
schwar-zen Wim-pern, sich in sanf-tem Wech sel ma-len!
pp
ppp
pp
pp wie in tiefes Sinnen verloren
Bles-sed Vir-gin's heav'n-ly child!
Sohn der Jung-frau, Him-mels-kind!
ppp
pppp